Gallery Books
Editor Peter Fallon
THE WAY IN

John McAuliffe

THE WAY IN

Gallery Books

The Way In
is first published
simultaneously in paperback
and in a clothbound edition
on 28 May 2015.

The Gallery Press
Loughcrew
Oldcastle
County Meath
Ireland

www.gallerypress.com

ISBN 978 1 85235 630 9 *paperback*
      978 1 85235 631 6 *clothbound*

A CIP catalogue record for this book
is available from the British Library.

The Way In receives financial assistance
from the Arts Council.

Contents

for Nancy

'But if that Land be there, quoth he, as here,
And is their Heaven likewise there all one?'

Very

It's a colour
        it's walking in the dark
It's the road
It's a car we drove
        it's crying
alternately to
        it's trying
work and holidays
        it's a small dog you loved to juggle on your foot
In cities it's the beach
        it's a night
it's a glass of wine
        it's the morning and the radio
in a small glass
        saying something out loud, oblivious
There is more
        it's mid-afternoon, once in a while,
        it's very
        it's very you

Shed

for Peter Fallon

I bought the shed, for a song, off a neighbour
who'd stopped using it after he paved the garden.
He'd inherited it or got it somewhere he couldn't remember,
not that I gave a second thought to its origin.

It was heavier than it looked so he helped take the roof to
    pieces.
After an hour prying out each crooked tack
we levered off its grey-green sandpaper stiffness
and rested it, on the drive, like a book stranded on its back.

The neighbour, looking at his watch, said, 'Let's push',
and the four walls and floor did move — a little.
In front of the garage, sweating, feeling each
ounce of the previous night, we saw too late

it was too big to go through. We counted the nails but couldn't:
they were like stars, more the more we looked. 'Heave it over,'
over the garage and down, he joked,
the garden path to its resting place under the magnolia.

No joke: we made a ramp of the ladder and inched
this half-tonne pine crate up and out of the road.
The scraped-flat garage roof pitched
under our careful feet. Two euphoric beers later, after we'd
    lowered

it into place, we agreed on twenty quid. Every so often
he still calls in: today he's selling up and getting out.
He asks about the shed. I say it's fine, so half hidden
by April gusts of leaf and petal he can hardly see it,

as we look, out the window, at where it leans
against the fence, painted green, the unlocked door
opening on the lawnmower and half-full cans
of paint and petrol, pure potential, evaporating into the air.

But work makes work: paving the lot, he volunteers, makes
    more sense.
I'm offering him a cup of tea
when, before he can collect himself, he starts to resent
the twenty quid and leaving the shed behind: 'It was,' he says,
    'almost free.'

The Retreat

for Lucy and Jerry

1

A quiet house with, once
in a while, sirens.
An office, the computer
hooked to a printer

and offline. A white wall
and a desk with nothing on it at all
except what I put there. This. The bell
of that church, clean and punctual.

Not diggers, or a road crew,
a mobile's humming or even
a party. No books, newspapers. No one
complaining about hours. And the view?

High Street. A newsagent, a nail bar.
The post office that's part of the Spar
and the Spar that's part of the off-license
I won't drive past — is that the hour? —

to the out-of-town shopping centres.

2

Jangle the hangers in the empty wardrobe.
Size up the flaws in the mirror.
Shift wrinkled clothes from the suitcase to the paper-lined
drawer.

A hair in the twelfth chapter of a long American novel;
one picture on the mantelpiece at a different angle,
a girl looking down at her Scottie, with a parasol.
That's all.
The cleaner, though she doesn't look it, is professional.

All week the bluebottles I've gone after
with a folded-up newspaper
buzz still, *buzz buzz*, above the desk and up and down the flat.
Until today, coming back from a long dinner,
I swat them, not with the paper but the Bloodaxe Neruda,
splat, or a sound very like that. And that.

3

Mist lifts from the yard's gravel pit.
Planted bushes
look like birds' nests, and host
unplanned, half emerged visitors,
one a cat, and a couple

holding hands, chancing their arms,
the yard a slow motion arena
they crunch, one alongside the other,
absorbing the heat of the sun.

The whole place is empty, waiting.
Voices carry into it,
someone shouting from the kitchen,
'Your problem is you don't listen.'

4

A day nothing will darken:
in the shaded kitchen
a space clears as the leaf
of the table is lifted level.

And what is it in the silence
that appears? 1985, sand, towels
draped across the chairs,
her voice, arranging the place,

Ambre Solaire, his big shoulders
painfully hot and shedding skin
which rubs off as it is handled
or, under my fingernail,

peels away in thin,
papery patches. Sheer,
blurring wing-scraps
I look through.

Stand-off on Santiago Street

for Luke Yates

When I run into you you're belting past
on your ex-postie's bike, a flyer
alongside my bullbar hybrid.
I'm bombing home, the school run, you're
on the way in, PhD on Catalan squatters
almost but not yet quite out of
your capacious bag. Different hours,
and directions, and the street we halt at,
in the shadow of the uni, the usual cross,
elderly immigrants driven demented
by subdivided sublet student ruins. I point out,
or you do (we are natural pointers),
the pick-up truck with its wheelless car
on the flatbed under a tarp. I'd never,
I explain, seen the pick-up move,
or the car on its back change; but no, most weeks,
you say, it's a different car under its blue tarp,
the man does business and the business is not —
as I think, about everything — a front. You change
the subject, you lived around here once . . .
                                        A week ago, I say,
police bothered a family while a body,
under a blanket, was stretchered out
to an ambulance. I'm freewheeling,
though I see you have to be away. And my kids
in the emptying yard will be looking at their feet.
But, one more: another time a man screeched
his banger of a Micra to a stop, right here,
not half a block from where a couple
stood talking. Half in, half out of the Micra,
engine still beating, he roared, maybe *shrieked* is better,
'I fuckin love ye Louise', then pulled the door to,
making no move, right after being so carried away.

By Fire

Among hundred-windowed blocks
smoke falls, drifts in
and out of trees, now rises up,
grey and beige furling

at the wind's direction
in tiny, paler ribs,
gusting again, making hollows
a perspective:

everything to which
a life is faithful, burning,
falls into place around
its disappearing breath.

The Unofficial Dead

Poems for David Gledhill's 'Dr Munscheid' Project

1

Beckmann, formally dressed in St Louis,
raises a foaming champagne glass.
He raises that flute
to a Romanov taxi driver and a Jewish haberdasher,
our Iraqi interpreter
saluting the Irish seamstress and bitching about the gypsy
    lion tamer.

2

The new furniture takes a turn.
It stars in the empty sitting room.

3

Upstairs, the doll-like child
in her pooled nightie
plays with dolls:
what a life they live
on the stand-in bed-cum-world,
the light shining on the distant pillow
like untranslated fiction.

4

Peering away from one photo
on his way into another,

or sprawled in a tub chair,
drunk, tie between 6 and 7 o'clock,

round glasses dug into
the round, clocked face;

manning the fancy-dress parade
in his ambulance cart,

fur hat and frilly parasol,
smiling at his screwdriver:

static, varnished, at our mercy,
new man, veteran baby.

5

Each day is wound up like a clock
though it is a different student who observes,
alongside the diffident dachshund,
the racing pages give way to the girls, the girls
and the stumbling pause of the bear
which walks into the bar ring-ringing a bell . . .

Cover

1 WHAT WE SAW

The setting sun's reflection sailing towards us, a distant cliff's
pink terrace tilted on the water whose ghost ships fade
into the sandy green; ice cities, churches, an aqueduct; up
   close
the shepherd's dog is half leopard, half sheep, the birds bats;
the fisherman has been drinking and another bird,
too large and red-eyed for its branch, looks out
from a shadowy corner that seemed, as we looked, to refer to
   our arrival.
The shepherd faces the empty tree. The peculiar backstroke,
Icarus disappearing into centuries of waves,
is played onto the water behind him. The ship's hands,
past masters of the averted gaze and redundant detail,
have their backs to us and the wind pushing them out to sea.

2 ROUND AND ABOUT

Much delayed by faulty trams and a misread sign we're halted,
outside the museum, by a smashed TV on the footpath,
fallen from who knows what heights, its screen
a glittering edge on red wire and green and silver circuits,
its crocked, fallen, akimbo openness
a guess at how that morning it entertained the gathered family
for an hour, in Dutch, while — on our way — we walked
   bitter squares,
buying bread and milk and photographing iced-up fountains,
you out of focus in your scarf, looking away at the elaborate
railed windows, the art nouveau roofs and doorways.
The casing we slowly left behind, with backward glance
and upward look at its unlikely origin. No need
to go around stating the obvious, about endurance, or time:
something landed, out of nowhere, out of the ordinary,

through the same shaking light in which, later, at the *Sortie*,
diving for cover and catching up, everyone
and his mother waits for us, subtitles
disappearing into speech and proffered umbrellas.

3   FAMILY ROOM

Here we are, the family room, my back-to-front
'Intro to Litho' coming up, as you might expect,
as 'something' blue squeegeed into a frame
while you stage-manage the kids into an elegant line,
no longer the groom and bride, rosily afloat
over Russian peasants, nor yet the shark tanked and split,
nor those longing companions Poussin
stitches into the fringes of a citified garden,

though skipping the exhibition after, max, an hour
I see under the electrifying, blue-black velvet
umbrellas of an Impressionist underwriter,
a sudden, first look we occasionally visit.
Traffic can snarl all it wants around its blue.
In case you're ever wondering, I want to.

The Mud Pump

Dogs, placards and mud.
The long vehicle stalls
a mile down the turn-off
from the ship canal slip road:
stacked, overloaded, stuck
on the map at Barton Moss,
a country lane, and ages
from where, feet up
and useful as a dropped pin,
I'm looking over
(the signal cabled to
and from a server farm)
homemade WordPress sites
and Smith's 'delineation
of strata' (1815),
mining the bumpf
and finding names
for what the creviced
earth might yield
when it's fracked,
then packed with sand
and dense and dry as the moon . . .
The truck, then trucks,
under a new law, flatten
lane and placard.
A well pad pipes
the water down, then out,
radial and horizontal,
beneath the field
of held-up camera phones
and the shifting
greys and blue above.
Pictures of what?
I upload the mud pump,
its spider's head and book

lung, hollow legs
invisibly rooting
into the rock; change,
exchange, new life
plumbed into the stone.

A Pebble

On the lane to the beach
between high hedges
the sounds turn dense,
internal: humming bees,
hushed green, a blackbird
and, that once,
the palm tree in a gap,
click-trickling in the breeze.

Cow parsley, dandelions,
brambles, nettles and docks.
Sandflies, horseflies, a pebble
sunk between the tide's salt lines,
the comet tail of its sandy descent
spiralling behind it,
like the names for things,
a bite raising a lump on my finger.

Look up. The sea and the sky
are the same blue.
Not discovery, that afternoon
we couldn't stay. More like
something remembered.
Offshore a boat, without a horizon,
appeared to drift
into its own reflection.

It surfaces, somehow, months later,
when hail, deflected
off the glass, briefly heaps
on the car roof, a hopping inch
rain pours on after,
a softening sequence. And an erasure
as it sprinkles, pools, steadies
and plays notes

on what it slants off,
the hedge, a trike, the car and sill,
slow, fast, and down the drains,
nothing irrelevant
to its decimal point accuracies . . .
The night, behind its trailing off, a tap
running dry. Dark matter
in the comet's streamy tail.

Echo

                              Pushing open the porch door
on what has nested behind it these many days,
it scrapes and catches as I bend down and away from
the milk bottles and bins to pick up the red cards
for missed deliveries, multiple copies of the 'local' paper,
our MP's updates on cuts and parking,
takeaway offers and the glittering remnants of a gift
dropped on the tiled floor the night before I left

for Lisbon, sandcastles, a wave washing up on the shore,
buckets and spades, a puff of air in the high places,
ice-cream cones, a month coming closer and closer
to the end of its power, a celloish withdrawal
from the porch's altering air finding me at a loss,
patting jeans as the house key does not appear —
where is it I would be going? or getting away from?
(a geography precise and confining as a childhood

that each inching away extends and deepens) —
no key emerging from under a mat or out of a pocket,
getting a laugh from knocking on my own door,
but not so much when, stepping out
to peer in the window, it sounds, on the other side,
as if someone's typing, the kettle's steaming and the drum
of the washing machine is rattling to, its wilful belting on
followed by beeping, as if I've been, these many days, an echo

right here really, of a life that has gone on, regardless,
beyond the floral spheres and bee violins August sucked
into a green square, its timbre and treble these many days
met by the industrial hum which worsens, cut with
that pejorative roaring that won't admit another,
the radio in the kitchen going on about what lies in store,
its right-or-wrong, 'must be done', parental decibel
shouting down and amplifying what it would correct,

as I right myself in the draughty porch, locked out,
my silence a rail I would ride away from it.

Let's.

The Coach House

She's breathless, stuck, stooped
below her wheeled frame, not
able, it turns out, to reach the clippers,
one gardening glove still on.
The brambles had raised their heads
outside the window of the coach house,
the coach house her husband,
just before he'd died, converted
so as to suit their old age better. Now
the bushes and grass and brambles,
the least of her problems, grow up
unruly about what he had planned.
Three weeks ago — she's still *in* time —
her legs gave out. But she thinks
she can do what it turns out she can't.
The front step is an obstacle and the clippers
she somehow screwed together
open on the doormat. The blades
are back to front, they grip but don't mark
the brambles' branching strength. I make her
a cup of milky tea, reverse the blades. She tires
of talk — changes in the city, how builders
exploited her dying husband —
and, cutting off enquiries about life before,
she rights herself in her chair again,
saying thanks and, as she looks at the shears
I left on the counter near the unopened post,
explains she must lock the door after me
and, struggling with her glove, asks —
on my way out — would I slip this spare key
under the mat, or keep it somewhere safe.

Longford Park

for Vona Groarke

The pavilion's deserted
and grass creeps
out of tarmac tennis courts.
Someone's been at the hedges.

An Afghan hound,
off the leash, on the loose,
lopes towards pigeons
and a blackbird. Dusk

and the gates close
on the last jogger. A minibus
turns on its lights
and heads for the city.

Over the south wall,
in the hidden garden,
the top of a bouncy castle
and, every so often, children.

Wild

Waiting. For a call, for news. Digging around.
Sitting on a log, next to the stump it was sawed from,
which is holed and host to vacillating flies.
Not a word all week. Stuck, thought trailing thought,
ivy growing around an eggshell; pine needles and holly,
cured brown by summer heat, falter into the moss. No

inner resources. Noise from the water is the pike's
slash at the surface and its dumping itself into the depths.
With nothing to do, easy to notice, bluer as they dock,
long-tailed dragonflies festering among the sallies
that spring out of the marsh. A bird shadow
shifts across the leaves. Swans, maybe *wild swans*,

(wild, you hear her say, because they are not *old*),
tow one another across the placid, hovered-over lake.
They leave the shallows, which hold the sky more truly,
for that far-out weave the fish disturbed:
opaque, glittering, its million rapid points of light
short the lines. Fishbowl, skybowl, giving me a signal.

From Here

The view from here is the border:
the lake, close-up, is vertical.
Not so much water as law and order.

The word for it might disappear,
the road run through its invisible wall.
The view from here is the border

vanishing around an otter,
swallows, tractor, trailer and damsel-
fly, not so much law as a stretch of water.

Mind your footing on its thin air.
There's the fault whose tremor you feel.
The view from here is a border

gone over and over, a fact of nature,
an impression that's begun to snowball,
not so much water as law and order,

a wavering queue, a detention centre,
a dotted line turned block and fractal:
the view from here is the border,
law and order written on water.

Film Set on Earth

Unforced, off set, the sound man
turns to his neighbour and asks for a light.
Inside, for us or someone like us, the crew is shadowy,
huge around the klieg light's spotlight.

Unforced. The roses. The sound man smoking.
The girl putting away her noisy light.
The kitchen, small, wooden, narrow, from which she emerges
with tea to sit in the TV light.

Every starting point prefigures its ending.
But to look is to miss the tears that alight
on the faces of everyone who has ever known her,
the fever of her growth into the light.

On Earth

At the bus stop under the horse chestnut, we tally the length
  of *Boyhood*
against the babysitter's plans for later and, waiting,
see the leaves have started to wilt,
brown at their July edges, losing a little of spring's climb
  upward;

afterwards, emerged from the dark into a thunderstorm, we
  see out
the tree's arching welcome to spikes of lightning,
its base flooding,
growing into reduced circumstances, swelling up, but still
  about.

Is this what it means to be someone? I'm not saying anything,
but twenty-four hours later, the smell in the air is of rain drying
  off stone, *petrichor*,
the tree's slow and seasonal evaporation. A way of answering

to a day, to years of them, that we step into and speak up for.
To you.
There is no one else I am talking to.

Soft Landing

What will I be wearing?
A suit and tie, good shoes.

Rouge.
And an attempt at lipstick.

Will I have my glasses on?
And where will it rest,

this made-up body? Who with? My father
taking me to his mother's, 'among what rushes'

on the far side of a new motorway.
We'd visit by walking across a field,

in a hurry till after, leaving Imphrick,
and not really seeing what she's missing.

Common ground. And for company?
I know. Morbid thought

forming around a star,
your hard fire:

I would be, now or at the hour,
in the dark alone first, counting that

another success:
Breathe the air and smile at this.

Reading this on the back of a letter
found in a shoebox in the shed
next to the wooden garden table
I've screwed back together for the summer.

The paper's creased carefully
at the folds, much considered once
but never sent from here
or copied, just put away

where it stirs in the shadow
of the unkillable linden,
lopsided and ragged
as if it's growing out a haircut:

a magpie — the national bird,
opportunist, a noise abroad —
perches on the table,
then on a skinny branch,

unsteady gauntlet it jumps off,
clambering among sweet spots,
soft landings, eager for light, forgetful
even in departures.

Home, Again

for Conor O'Callaghan, Evan Jones and Ian McGuire

Then want I words to speake it fitly forth
                    — Spenser, 'Colin Clout's Come Home Again'

I THE RED LION

The regulars agree the cheesy ritzes beat the crisps
and someone sings the praises of Wisdom, Norman
Wisdom. 'You would have to hold it against anyone who didn't
have a liking for him or,' he coughs, 'for George Formby of
    Formby . . .'

Talking peters out as glasses empty and we circulate like
    clock hands
from bar to loo to this corner table's cardinal point. Then work
    arises.
Writing much? We are. I even brought some. Sheets I laboured
    over
and now surround with talk of what it is I wasn't doing.

Then you drop your bombshell. You're returning. It's not
what it was, when the 'crew that used to be' brought the reader
and the critics flocking, wondering that the ancient art
had found a mouth and pulse. If there is no soloist like him
    who's gone

there's still the old choir coming in at the chorus, and that squall
of feedback that lets you know that something happened. And
    now?
Is there something to be said for us, this shower, this avalanche
of poet-critics, pol corrs, stand-ups, lecturers and journalists in
    verse?

Who's to say, either way! — though there are times our antic
devotion to tracking one another's online manoeuvring would
    make
an angel blush and one who loved the art believe it is
coming to a dying, awful, lazy end, its energies, such as they
    are,

devoted to the greasy poles monkeys nimbly clamber up, fools
outdoing one another in the round of summer schools,
    committees,
prize juries, uni networks a lunatic would run a mile from . . .
''Twas ever thus,' you say. 'Next thing, you'll be at openings
    yourself.'

'If that's the world, there as here, why,' I ask, 'go back to it?'
'I'll steer well clear of that,' you say, 'what'd you think this
    summer past?'
'I drove all over and all seemed to be doing OK, but it's
    strange now
where I go and what it is I see, or maybe how I see it. That's
    what,'

I point to this sheaf, 'I've spent these three years working on',
    a term
it's understood does not count teaching or organizing school
    runs or how
to put an audience before a writer, or building up
an archive of to-do lists in the precincts of a marriage I won't

for once go into detail on, to whose happy storms I will return.
    All this
when I wasn't halfway up this greasy pole I'm perched on here.
I ask the bar for another round of bitters, and crisps,
and clear my throat and begin to try these redrafts out.

2 THE VALLEY OF THE BLACK PIG

The trestle sags, right there
where the pig's big perfect head,
hugely perched on stalky, flat-out forelegs,
unbalances the stretcher.

The stripy-aproned cook
cuts soft fatty meat from its back
onto the paper plates we line up with,
looking it in its char-black eye.

The festival, the feast, is built
around the return,
after years away, of a successful son.
There's a hashtag, a website

and a temporary structure
in the school playground,
a North Kerry weekend
his New World mates signed up for,

going to town
on the *hangi* details.
The all-age crowd circles
the pit: no Maori stone

in the bog, so they fired metal,
an iron gate, old tractor parts
in a furnace, then put
the lot, iron, coal and all,

into the earth. The chef:
'We wrapped it in wet

jute sacking, with cabbage,
buried it here last night.'

The men dig down, hot work
as they strip off their shirts;
a couple of young ones baulk,
covering their mouths

as the animal
in a cloud of heat
emerges from the earth,
arriving among us, its people,

an image
for the front page of the paper,
returned to our language
like a king on his stretcher.

3 RUIN 2 (SAT NAV VERSION)

Arriving in the dark, a low satellite gleams
like a high window beyond the orchard.
It has ideas about how things are
and, once in a blue moon, returning,
not sure where I am, things
glitter and twinkle with an underwater look,
every high wall legible as crevice, foxhole,
breathing space, so nothing seems, for an instant,

outside its pale and wholly comprehending mouth,
like the well-bred voice which would correct
every accidental left or right,
until I start to make out, by its light,
the overgrown entrance to the house,
summer retreat turned safe house and symbol.
Hard, escaping the swim of work,
not to fall for its big picture, bumping into

the glassy fact of slow thought
becoming a long life. It lights up
around the sagging, blu-tacked A4 sheet headed
OPW and the sign for visitors
which bars entrance to the tower's kitchen garden
whose apples are dry and sweet.
In the long grass shadows falter where a path breaks in,
flattened stalks unbending, the matted way

dipping every so often to the brown river
no one steps in. It brought us here, the satellite.
It might last forever, a sort of
Anglo-Norman, laying down a route
for which the old map is no help, its flash
visible from the black and watery meadow

that keeps being gone back to, the old names
hovering behind its aspirations.

4 SWANS

The arc of the driveway is what's left,
where someone built a house and tended a lake
to walk beside, discussing politics
and how a tree moves in the wind. Its music
is a jetty drifting away from the boathouse
whose rolled-shut metal door tricks
visitors into thinking it holds a life raft.

The house drifts beyond its purpose,
is demolished for a car park and picnics
and returns in a special room, small, sturdy,
becoming anonymous as its windows empty,
enormous insects swanning around — they own the place —
occasionally stunning themselves on the glass.

5 SECRETARIAL

The country, sometimes, still appears to ask
    to just be taken down, even by a tourist, on no one's side,
    a tourist lost at home, blue book open, ticking off each task.
But when old Colin, in pyjamas, explained how I could evade
    the barbed and electric wire that fenced off fields
    and the bull let loose to scare the stranger off
    (I'd stopped to ask for directions), I was ready to wade
    through cowshit and knee-high grass to see if
the poet, long abroad, was written in the ruin's native life.

Colin stopped me then, leaning on the open door of the
    Renault —
    noting first the English registration
    I'd parked outside his roadside bungalow,
    and said his father hated that his mother called him *Colin*,
but he's the one who stuck it out. No one,
    it seems he had to tell me this, no one belonging to them
    ever had
    to go over to England, a sally he follows up with a question
about where I live, before naming the man on whose land the
    castle rested:
    we do nothing, he says, but damage what we inherited,

bulldozing the medieval church and causing the collapse
    of the foxhole the settler and his family used, legend has it,
    to make, under a smouldering fire, their escape.
    This new heir has his eye on the castle, no doubt.
It will soon be more literature than history. We are not
    all the same, he said. I recall, at the edge of the clearing,
    the grant's nice clause saying the poet had a right
to possess new areas discovered by his survey . . . To *belong*,
    a moment's authority is nothing.

6 DMZ

After dropping a guest to the airport,
host itself that day to a planeload of marines
en route to somewhere awful,
I drove quickly away till, needing a walk,
I stopped off the N24 and parked
in the triangle opposite the tourist office,
a redone kitchen, on a footpath
that was more lintel than path.
First stop, the Knights Templar tower,
a grassy ruin overlooking the grave
of de Vere, whom a century of poets treasured.
An old man, smoking, followed me in

and out by the noisy gate for the castle,
attacked, he approached to tell me,
in the plantation of 1567,
and unrecovered or used since then,
its huge stone ruin preserved and gated,
as if it were something.
A mile down the flat brown Deel,
the deserted friary founded
a century after Francis' death
is similarly roofless
but has delicate thin-spoked chancels,
gravel lining its run of chambers,
graves like plants in its unlikeliest corners
and graffiti etched onto its chimney breasts,
new poetry lichened but,
speaking like lead in marble,
louder than the tourist office

which closed for the day at half four,
the woman staffing it walking away,

the paper under her arm.
Half a millennium after the sack of the town,
its terraces collapsing, one pub sells jewellery
and next door, in another, the butcher,
stopping for a drink with two identical brothers,
hears that a man, last night, shot pellets
at three others sitting in a stationary car,
then chased them off towards the castle
where he sprayed them again. The butcher
is all business, says he knows the shooter,
and also the deserters who should be barred.

About to reverse out of town I see
two Indian guys who have come a long way
to carry a frying pan and oil to Kwik Bites,
where the old smoker waits by the counter
with the names he half recognizes
scratched into the veneer: Madonna, Aidan,
CIRA, Eminem, MH♥SOS, and other
notorious outlaws.

7 BY NIGHT IN BALLY

What if we raise the tenth wave
and reduce the coast to a sieve?
Outside the big stars of another era
will shine vague as ice in vodka.

The swell from the deepest harbour
will ease into its granite neighbour,
nests of swing and slide
crumble from the cliffs' sunny side.

Like the drink making slush of its ice,
rounding its edges, dotting its dice,
what if there's no way to start over
and the night's mixed into the future —

everyone's a prophet about this —
the bar is as clear as fizz
till the last drop, the whole lot, tips
in a moment to these moving lips.

8 NOWHERE, INT

We couldn't hear, above the eastbound traffic jam, the V of
    geese,
or see in this evergreen outpost a local branch of any kind.
High Street in the midlands. Stalled, where the *shore*
    disappears.

The harvest festival amps up, roadside, covers of rock classics
that, year round, hum off the radio: Aerosmith, U2, Queen.
Queue at the portaloos (or use the petrol station). Beyond the
    geese

the moon makes a brief appearance. Proper order. We salute it
and remember the double rainbow we drove under,
hours earlier, in the Glen of Aherlow. 'Arlo'. The other world

in this one. Then wingflaps sudden as water,
and we're away again. Wipers going. Now you like
the idea of standstill; and so do I, looking back, inland, once
    in a while.

9 NATIONAL MONUMENT

That morning, scrabbling away at the ground,
imagine him scratching his head, imagine the thing
as he found it, setting off the illegal, wired-up stick
with its plain metal basin. Nothing important,
he might have said to himself, digging away, don't mind us,
this beer can's not nine inches underground, until . . . *Now now*,

he tells himself. Shouldn't be here he knows, but he'll know
as well the myth (a golden gate half hidden underground)
and the fact of Ardagh's turning up the other chalice.
He *had* set out, informally, to unearth *something*,
crossing the bog to the little island, the 'national monument',
where the ruins of the monastery are stuck,

not knowing that morning how stuck
the find would make him. Rubbing the muck off it anyhow,
he couldn't have reckoned what the treasure meant.
Never *his*, it's an opencast mine for judges digging around
for ways to drive every calf back to its cow, a precedent earthing
the future . . . And when he seeks a return on the chalice

(worth six million will be the market advice),
the museum reward, by court order, is stuck
at 10k which, at that time, is not nothing
but is no one's idea of a killing. Not when you know
the old church would have remained undisturbed ground,
its interest entirely legendary until he went,

freelance, into the ruins and came out a curator by accident.
Before that February morning the chalice —
useless, unlamented index to roofless grounds,
cutaway bog and looted graves — was set to be stuck

on that absurd island on the far side of the bog even now,
full to its lip with a world it is dead to, an inarticulate thing,

its ladle, tray and spun silver stand gone for nothing,
likewise his name, and the life's work in each interlaced dent,
experts judging its form first *Insular*, then *Viking*, or arguing now
about why so few beasts decorate the chalice,
or suggesting a monk, and not a thief, originally stuck
the lot, before he died or was killed, into the honest ground

where it *keeps*, the underfoot chalice, unknown, moot object
of drawn-out legal argument, its undiscovered life struck
off, vanished, imagine, into its proving ground.

10 COLIN, AGAIN

'"*Then want I words to speake it fitly forth*":
an idea, a name that will forever be entwined
with whatever crap is written on the counter
or scrawled around the graveyard walls
or scraps of initials and three-hit bands
inscribed on bins by bored and mitching schoolkids.
Who'll write of this as well, when write they do:
it will come into the things they'll dearly name,
fields, animals, the house they marry into and their child,
and that child's children too will know some guise
of this engraved idea I speak of now: POETRY,
the language drawing us out of ourselves,
hollow boon, vacuum, a screen
projecting onto us shades we call our own
which flicker on, as we do and don't intend, redoubled
in a story told across a table or on a walk
among the fields whose stony decorations
we ignore and marvel at alternate days,
even you who hear this song today, rambling off
through acres no one we know has ever owned.'
'What has that do with keeping house,
a pint, the match, or who did what to whom?'
'It's the place through which those things can pass,
guttering, into the hard fire we truly see them by.
Someone says I should go and live there, *in* the fire,
rather than annoying them back here,
but it doesn't work like that, it's what comes and goes.'
Now he speaks with what the poet calls 'celestial rage'.
'I prefer to the stone the river's repetitions
that swim into view like a premonition
which is also déjà vu: we'll remember the Flood
as the waters rise up around our waists,
(the eel and the roach mistaking us for what?).

Over and over a discovered heaven, the first kiss,
the other world that is not all it's cut out to be . . .'

11 BY NOW

The sun blazed and we loaded up the blue Fiesta,
drove east, your father's van gone first and racing us,
whether we liked it or not, on to and off the ferry.
In a cheap hotel I lost my mobile, not for the last time.
We searched for our new address like children
who dig through a box of fancy dress, dense and jammed
until prying fingers disclose a costume —
superhuman cape and gauzy veil — they mostly wanted.

We'd crossed the sea and a dozen rivers to find
a roundabout with a pub on the corner, The Ox,
a post office next to a deli, a steep hill,
a station, Mill Hill East, we would vote at, once,
where I'd board every morning, ignoring the papers
ignored by our Ashkenazi and Farsi neighbours,
trundling out of the sunshine, eating the shit
I was fed and calling it manna from heaven.

Emigrant, optimist, disowning the borders
we didn't see ranging around us like axe heads,
every word out of our mouths someone else's.
Catching up, trailing rainclouds, ambushed
by the Dutch heat of an English summer
which knew our fathers worked at the roads
driven through suburbs that widen year on year,
splashing cash on what's coming next,

the place *change itself*, changed, hardened, or it was us,
changed by them, changing them. We were,
we are what we brought with us, it's still
the rivers, old machines, the tunnels, steep hill
and costumes carrying us where we'd never been,
looking up from the map we'd borrowed,

a tractor and trailer blocking off the horizon
on the road from Doneraile to Kilcolman, asking the question.

A terrace in Moss Side with Esther Roper
and, for cover, her brother, redbrick outreach and 'sex
is only an accident'. Join the union. Workers
knew her, who she was, and didn't care:
one of the Gore-Booths, who hears the 'dearer
waves of Breifni' . . . If she walks out Booth Street,
Lissadell's there: its western coast

is part of her position, but the town
is her arena, an outpost of the future.
She is her sister's keeper, and guardian
of the acrobat, the gymnast,
barmaids, flower-seller and waitress, no, waiter,
writer, teaching poetry at the Round House
on Every Street, driving a coach-and-four

up a dry woodland path not just anyone can enter,
where a bust of Lenin and a portrait of Napoleon
settle down in a biggish house, in the ante-room,
like characters from her *World Pilgrim*
sharing a sick joke about what used to happen
in the garden, in the belvedere. Strike!
This wasn't the teddy bears' picnic.

And now? A semi in the suburbs lets the terrace. Digs,
through which strange life passes, 19,
20, 21; the former factory, *Hans Knit*,
is a mosque with tall weeds and a Friday crowd,
laced trainers and starlings on a redundant line.
Everyone around is mobile: rooms, services,
blow, change hands for half nothing, more or less.

On Heald Place junk and parcel, will
and codicil, pile up, 'not known at this address'.
Dreaming up a subject, knock the walls
about an iron bed on which nothing's built
and Urania is to be found. Free
and silent now as a hand reaching out for a waif,
'more, more', its dream double as constant as life.

13 THE WAY IN

At one o'clock the old men and at three o'clock too.
At four o'clock a stone stairway and the sea,
old airs and the lure of a fiddle in an echoing hall.
At six the window, fixed, and with a green sill:
what's done and said is clear from the bare table
at which the men sit. At eight the bar, which will go
till ten, then a tower, the introduction of a border
and the extended home whose courtyard a swineherd crosses.
In the hallway velvet gloves, water bottle, a black lace fan
embroidered with ghost orchid and dog rose; inside,
a sofa from the '90s parked by an image of a boggy little stream,
whose names and days are numbered in a plan
I'm looking up from: almost midnight and there are things
right here for which there are, as yet, no instructions.
The door, the boat, the way out the only way in.

14 THE WAKE

'Struggling for wifi, scanning emails
about one thing and another — the new semester
and my good friend's wife's diagnosis:
I get him on the phone,
arranging to meet for a drink when I'm home,
where the pain is, and its intensest opposite.'

I finished that before I came out (having started it another
     night,
leaving Croker early for a ferry
that stalled for hours in high winds
just off Holyhead,
which is where I made up what follows):
A drink for the road. And take this away,

I'm not taking it anywhere else. It isn't
a state of the nation, or of
'contemporary mores'. It's trying to be straight,
ish, but nothing side-of-the-mouth —
nothing to google! When you go back, how's this?,
tell me how it looks, there. Tomorrow?

It's for running off tonight. All I'll be able for.
Going left at Oak Road,
up Circular, then Palatine, Lapwing Lane,
slow across Wilmslow,
where the cars will be parked
on the footpaths I'm pounding, on into Fog Lane

to lap duckpond, dilapidated rosebeds,
vandalized playground
and the multiplying football pitches, then out by Old
     Broadway,

slow across Wilmslow,
with a glance north to the Red Lion
dodging the 42s, thinking about a book I started, home again.

15 EPILOGUE

Goodbye, I said, stirring from sleep —
I was leaving, so the city's streets and weeks,
side roads and greens and years turned overnight
into a single place, a city I knew as one park:
lifting my head from the desk
where years of notes pile up, altogether all at once,
I could see it like an engineer, cordoned off,
with his finger on the detonator button
early in the milky morning light of May.
The sky lit up like a glass of water
I raised to the world as I suddenly knew it,
the place changing again, superfast, as I chose it,
stirring from sleep, Goodbye, Goodbye.

Montevideo

after Jules Supervielle

I was being born and at the window,
passing by, was the horse pulling the plough

in from the brightening edge of the far field,
a mosaic which tile by tile the light revealed.

Who was driving it? Whoever was up
woke the day with a little pop of his whip,

night's other element an archipelago afloat
above the day he had started,

walls raising themselves from the sand and cement
and river gravel that had waited in them, sleeping tight.

A little bit of soul, my soul, slipped by,
along a blue rail, a line in the sky,

and another bit folded itself
into a sheet of paper, under sail, adrift,

till it lodged under a stone,
its wildness caught and settled down.

The morning counted its birds,
never losing its place.

That sweet honeysuckle smell
gave itself to the morning's blue swell.

In Ireland, on the Atlantic,
the air was so affable, such a tonic,

that the colours of the horizon
came closer — to see the houses we lived in.

It was me being born, there where the woods almost speak,
on whose paths the grass grows, surely — but not too quick:
underwater, equally, seaweed and algae bob and wave:
the wind too will fall for them, they make believe . . .

Earth, always about to begin again its orbit,
recognizes us in its atmospheric dips,
feels, in the wave *and* in its profoundest deeps,
the swimmer's head, the diver's feet.

The Penny

I mustn't have sunk it in the water after I found it behind
   the shed
because here it is, the penny, back again in my pocket,
or it fell out anyway, so getting out of bed
it was there, shiny-eyed, on the carpet.

It's nothing, and don't make it into something,
just a penny, a little coin that wouldn't stick.
Don't make out it's a sign or has a meaning
like a bottle imp or some unquenchable storybook candlestick.

OK but did you see me try to give it away,
a tip for that terrible chowder we stopped for earlier,
by the lake, do you remember?, the day before yesterday,
and it came back staring up at me from the saucer.

I remember and the waiter's looking back at you as if
that were a tip. I'm getting up, I hear someone,
calling. Forget it. This is a holiday *and* there's enough
to worry about without this carry on.

I'll just leave it right here — no point, is there?,
in doing anything else and, after we've left
then we can see if it's all square,
if it stays here on the counter or if it *is* something daft;

you'll see, we'll turn around, a mile from the door,
for the camera or a toothbrush or *Battleship*
or a passport the kids made a game for:
if it's gone or makes it home before us will it be got-up

or if it looks up, becoming useless, from the dash as we
   embark,
what look will you shoot me in the below-decks dark?

Part of the Furniture

The door handles are stiff and squeak.
We empty a wardrobe, remove
a photo, files, a book she wanted,
and look around. The décor
is suddenly obvious, styles
that came and went, colours going
as late light pours
through the landing window
into what used to be your room.

No guessing, until we saw it,
that the child's rocking chair
lent, decades ago, by a neighbour,
would take on this heavy, amber permanence,
creaking, as soon as you touch it,
to and from a future
the day already darkens.

At a Concert

Throughout the ravishing sestet he composed poems.
                                        — Richard Outram

He reaches for a scrap of paper as the crowd files in,
fumbling it out of an overcoat beneath the flip-up seat.
The quartet, in their appointed places, tune up: he keeps
to himself the feeling this might be the part

he will enjoy the most. Tall, rumpled, all in black,
the composer is the image of a curate who kept him behind,
in the sacristy, one morning to count collection money.
The arresting opening bar strikes home and he feels

not at all bad, singled out even, though he worries
as the counterpoint continues, if that pain
coming into focus in his right eye is a scratch, he hopes not,
or a sty, which would be painful — he turns off his phone —

given the week he has ahead, the flights, there and back,
seeing his family, long journeys he'd like to read through.
But the half-stripped hallway and dented car, he arches his neck,
are on his mind and he wishes this passage would end

as he notices the light seeming to shift behind the cellist
gathered around her instrument like a slept-in coat,
and a familiar colour shines in the half lit front row
which he forgets, responding to the cellist's

sudden frenzied relieving response to the violins' permutations.
In Niagara once, by himself, he photographed the spray
and a boat that circled and almost tipped over, knowing
behind him stood gewgaw stalls from which he'd take
    something away,

thinking of this, as the applause starts, unprepared, eyes abrim,
someone had said, yes, there would be no interval,
so this was it, over before he was ready, and around him,
in the rustling coats, the shifting sounds of conversation.

The Rebuild

Walking upstairs into the dark —
they'd ripped out the electrics
to put in the new stairs —
she gripped where the banister had been

and tipped a little, as though she'd taken a drink,
or lost a heel, or aged overnight by years,
but steadying herself she went on
making another note of what must be fixed

and entered the plasterboard attic
which emerged from the dark as bins, papers,
a toolbox, a bucket of water with a half pint of milk in,
all half lit by the roof-opening Velux

and the fancier wall-mounted window — black,
argon-filled — which she'd known,
as she signed the cheque, she'd paid too much for
and knew now (as she stepped around the nails and tacks

that dotted the dust-thick floor)
were doing no good at all, letting in
not only the noise of the last birds flying back
to the garden's rowans and lilacs

whose waving branches she could hear
swaying in the late evening's cool sonics —
familiar, quiet, unpredictable music
above the shattered old roof on the unmown lawn —

but also, farther off, a bus's creaking brakes
at the stop a street away, hearing even,
the torch in her hand, the doors clatter open and the driver
name the price, there and back.

An Briathar Saor

Having cleared almost everything
we miss the piano and the bicycle on our return.
The piano went north, in a horsebox.
Not an ornament or even a photo is left
in the space where the sideboard has been.
The bed frames and mattresses are gone
from the bedroom where we ask
about the bike. A wheel will go east,
it's said, a pedal south, the chain west.
One story slopes away from another,
brother and sister, mother, father.
Put them together, you'll get the picture.

Swear

You know.
       The potholed lane
and spots of grass, a winding
and rewinding trail,
increasingly silent till,
just below the surface of the earth,
fleetingly visible,
the opening that draws me on,
wasting time.
       I have to go,
but now find another,
there before me,
who proceeds a while
at the same speed
till we look up
at where it all starts,
an oath, a *by whom*
and *in whose* I never
swore
       or was sworn to.
Shifting my weight from one
wrong foot to the other.
Say something, is it?

For Now

That sound wheeling in the corner,
            the over and over of the photocopier
and, opening an external door,
           smoke *and* fire
                somewhere north of here.

Household

Without disease, the healthful life;
The household of continuance
   — Henry Howard, Earl of Surrey

A bowl of water shakily reflects
the lilac in bud again,
the newly dug bed like a headscarf
small blackbirds dart from
to the sunlit tree,
stringing things along
before night slides in
among green leaves,
knowing no end
to their swaying to and fro,
the bright wind a table
at which I stand, again,
feeling a way into things.

Light dragging
its heels past six o'clock,
you offer, out the back door,
'First spring walk in the park?'
on your way,
knowing what I'm like.
Though the first wasp
flies straight back, for good,
into a hole in the wall
you're already stood at the cross,
making a cloud. The moon,
pitched low and thin, issuing
like steam from tea.
The trees, barely in leaf,
meet in shadows
on the finally shining roofs.

Before I say a word,
'Don't start,' you say. This
is unfinished spring,
close to the edge of things,
watch it, half green,
half petal-strewn, the lilac
budding penny-brown.
Our faces, look,
peer from the house's
black mirror at our first return.

It's not, is it?, as if this
never happened before,
the wind gusting
where the trees bud, the gate
shutting at later dusks
till parents shout
children's names
because it's time to go:
where the rain patters now
(I'm all for settling down
inside at last)
sand will glitter
on tarmac footpaths
cutting across inexplicable fields.

Astronaut

Sawing in half the cast-iron bath he says the house was built
  around
so that he can ship it, in parts, downstairs and out to the skip
  they've hired,
Neil, who is putting in the new electric shower, says to her,
  'The heating's
gone off now and the water too, but I'll come back later.'
  Climbing, *much* later, into bed
after her night on call in the freezing north, she starts to ask
  him, her husband, if Neil did,
return, that is, from wherever it was he went with the bath in
  pieces,

when she finds he is dead to the world with herself beside him,
  so begins
the careful, gravityless stepping around of an astronaut,
discovering on the bedside table, between 'how-to' books and
  the baby's bottle, the thermostat
he must have fallen asleep trying to reset, the temperature
  setting, as the unfolded booklet says,
unknown but, read by the alarm's red glimmer, closer to the
  second of its two settings,
not the one called 'Sun (or Comfort)', but 'Moon' which, it
  says, could be described as 'Off'.

A noise, in the pipes, the other side of the wall, where the old
  bath was,
that she ignores, along with the distractions of the rain and
  the state of the discarded floor,
a sea of disappointment it is as impossible to float away from
  as it is
to understand, in this light, at this hour, the word
  'Commissioning',

or performing the 'Initial power up' or asking, by the light of
     her phone, how to set the timer,
when it is too late to set the clock, everyone is leaving,

the door is shutting behind her like the set sun, and the idea of
     'comfort',
as she exits a week of nights for a week of nights, is not what
     anyone
is after in the shortening days they are aimed for . . .
Within one minute the old set values — she is turning in her
     sleep now — must be checked.
And there is no one to whom this can be reported. The
     equipment,
what's left of it, will persist. From now on, as before, she is on
     her own.

Downstairs, next morning, the house is warm, they're all out
     of bed.
He's put the thermostat in the fridge and boiled the last of the
     water with milk
for a restoring coffee: the big two are in their uniforms and
     ready for road;
by the skip in the drive he stands with the buggy, scarfed and
     gloved,
taking in instructions for the day ahead — what to say to Neil,
     we need milk,
what needs taking out of the freezer, when to call, all my love.

Knight

for Róisín, Ronan and Clíona

warlike arms, the idle instruments of sleeping praise,
were hong upon a tree
                              — Spenser

1 SWORD

He marches into the yard and calls all comers
in a flurry of blue and silver: he slips; he recovers;
he is the monsters he describes; roaring, he blinds
each foe, then mortifies or turns his enemies to stone; he finds,
in special cases, a new power, transmuting stone to dust
or, whirling anticlockwise, kills, with a spell, what moves too
    fast.
He lays out his charms and conquests in the porch,
a captive doll, a sheaf of horsetails, an old stopped watch,
then, saying nothing, presents to me his light sabre,
the blue tubing scuffed from the action, the handle's silver
not so worn I can't make out its outlined lightning bolt.
When I ask about the mess it's made he says it's no one's fault,
retracts the blue point so it looks like a relay baton
and, coming closer, makes as if to pass it on.

2 SHIELD

His shield he made himself, out of an old Amazon box,
having taken a kitchen knife to saw a heart shape out,
its edges rough, piped, serrated. He unrolled tin foil and tore,
papering the board with it and, from the sewing box, he took
two strips of red felt and fixed a cross to the shining foil.
Ready, after this ordeal of composition, craft and toil,
he made his way into the green yard and charged
but met, he could not believe his luck, the long broad axe

76

of the magnolia's lower bough, where the shield still hangs,
because as he pulled it back it seemed to snag and lodge
  there more.
Retelling the story after he had been disturbed — someone
  calling
as he dealt out busy pain — he mentioned drawing his magic
  wand
and making the whole green scene a whited-out pond or
  sepulchre,
forgetting that yesterday he'd told us all the wand was no more,
destroyed as he took issue with a neighbour in the rain
and that, as he spoke, it was easy to see over his shoulder,
the red and silver shield shining, in the sunset, from the tree.

3 CASTLE

When you've built, one domino on top of another,
a castle too small for your toy Palomino,
you wheel around, not seeing me
chopping up dinner in the kitchen,
as you turn back and begin.
The dolls are who you say they are:
friends at nursery *here*; us *there*.
You ask them, what should we play?,
and explain the days of the week and counting, to 110,
indicating your infinite exercise of dominion over time and
  space.
Then you dim the light. It's time.
In your conversation, a whisper, shining edges glitter.
You recite, 'Once upon a time, the end',
about to blow all into shadow,
trundling chaos towards the house.

4 EXEUNT

The dragon you find in the corner,
stranded on the hall's bare floor,
metal-winged, wheeled, tinily heavy,
calls vainly — 'Recycling', 'Charity' —
for you to come please and pick it up

till we find ourselves, the house asleep,
on our knees, putting the evening and years of practice
into pushing it between us, making plane noise,
mmmhmmm, nnnnng, ng, ng, nnnnng,
revving through take-off, bearing it all, up, up,
and no thought of landing.

Snail Days

Back and forth to town and ocean:
the train that takes us, snail days,
runs between like a thought,

a thought with rain streaking it
and fields like a faithful companion.
A swaying to which we listen,

coming, here and there, to terms
with the tide's systemic pulse,
the Atlantic silver like a city at night.

Lifeguard

Hours before you wake to my call
I walked out of the modular hotel
where not a soul could say
where anybody was and the 11th floor bar,
strip-lit and echoey, was closed.

Restless, numb, *underwater*
after the flight, I kept going, out and up,
via a superette to buy toothpaste,
the towers and highways a pre-dawn
dot to dot I walked into, till I saw the sun

rising over a coastal lido, its salt water
sprayed by a pulverizing southerly.
Even at this hour there's a lifeguard.
In shades, shorts and a black scarf, he has a couple
of little gulls, plus me, for company,

and the city below climbing thinly to his blue reprieve
from where the sea looks endless,
map-flat and patient as it slowly presses
into the built-up valleys, neglecting nothing,
a pylon in the shallows making waves

of daybreak. Though I can't, it turns out,
live everywhere, the light from the south
is an open door. I try it on (try harder!),
the gulls flying up out of the thought
that I go away to hear you say my name.

On Earth

One-offs, each drop formed about a speck of dust,
fall into the drying greenery of August.
Car doors clunk to, neighbours make their exit.
Summer and there's time to visit.
That time is now.
                    The flowers are an interest
we suddenly wish we'd taken since winter's blessed
the ground with cooler air and a hint of frost.

Summer we're about again to give up for lost,
hot and solitary as we dreamt it.

Embarked

a wooden Frame and Frail,
Glewed together with some subtile Matter

— Spenser

Finished with packing — the duvets
jammed around the cases in the boot —
I scour the usual corners for mobiles, chargers,
the book on non-space I never even opened,

racquets, bat, the frisbee
we hadn't the weather for,
and find, on top of a book of prayers
my aunty Mary gave the kids years back,

a stack of old CDs like an exec paperweight
on the study sill, some blank
except my brother's scrawl of dates
in blue permanent ink

counting backwards, summer ending early, again,
as I drive east, going faster
though it's *work* (pauses; forwards) playing it
between scratches. The port's fringe

slows to a shiny crawl; two boys
on a falling-down half-built site
are turning in and out
of a niggly, backs to the wall

one-on-one, like ours, with one 'goals'
a too tall b-ball net,
the other a gas cylinder,
and a mother now calling out

before one or other is finished off —
the clock reminding me to go
on board, not overboard, straggling in
to 'wash your hands', called

from where, between pillar and post,
something rolls,
the frame frail
under my unsteady instep. That feel.

House at Night

Because there's no one else around
you like the house at night.
Silent phones, a blank screen,
cherry blossom edging
the extra hour. Nothing to do.
No one's going to call.

                      Spring,
a forgotten pocket you dip into,
turns up a late ray of light
across your mouth
and neck.
House at night, last
a little longer!

Acknowledgements

Grateful acknowledgement is due to the editors and publishers of the following, in which many of these poems, or versions of them, were published first: *BBC3, Causeway/Cabhsair, The Cincinnati Review, The Dark Horse, Edinburgh Review, The Interpreter's House, Manchester Anthology, Map* (Worple Press), *Mimic Octopus, The Moth, New Walk, The North, Painful Moods, Partisan, Peter Fallon: Poet, Publisher, Editor and Translator* (Irish Academic Press), *PN Review, Poetry, Poetry International, Poetry Ireland Review, Poetry Review, The Rialto, Salamander, Sport* and *The Yellow Nib*.

A version of 'Echo' was commissioned as part of the sound artist Tarek Atoui's contribution to the Manchester International Festival's 'do it' show at Manchester Art Gallery in 2013.

I would like to thank the Tyrone Guthrie Centre at Annaghmakerrig where some of these poems were first drafted, and the Arts Council / An Chomhairle Ealaíon for a bursary in 2011.

I would not have been able to take advantage of opportunities for writing without the generosity of my family, and I have long benefitted, as has this book, from the friendly support of Peter Fallon, Daisy Fried, Vona Groarke, Evan Jones, Ian McGuire, Conor O'Callaghan, Maurice Riordan, Colm Tóibín and Jeff Wainwright.